Promises, promises

An Advent study course

NICK FAWCETT

Kevin Mayhew

First published in 2001 by
KEVIN MAYHEW LTD
Buxhall, Stowmarket, Suffolk IP14 3BW
Email: info@kevinmayhewltd.com

9 8 7 6 5 4 3 2

ISBN 1 84003 786 5
Catalogue No 1500451

Cover design by Jonathan Stroulger
Edited by Katherine Laidler
Typesetting by Richard Weaver

Printed and bound in Great Britain

Contents

To Alan and Beryl Chambers
and all at Chester Road Baptist Church
who, many years ago, showed me such kindness
during my student placement among them

Introduction

I have long felt there is a great irony in the way the Church celebrates Advent and Christmas. These are two of the most important seasons in the Christian year, rivalled only in significance by Holy Week and Easter, yet, we spend little time reflecting on what they have to say to us. If you're lucky, there may be one Sunday devoted to Advent themes, and after that, in many nonconformist churches at least (although I have been fortunate to worship in one of the exceptions), you'll most likely hear nothing more than a brief homily until the week after Christmas, worship being given over to nativity and Christmas carol services. Such services, of course, have become a traditional part of our celebrations, and I for one wouldn't want to change that, but what compounds the situation is that house-groups, midweek meetings or Bible studies similarly tend to adjourn in mid-December to allow time for Christmas parties, carol singing and the like. The result is that we tend to explore the Advent and Christmas message in less depth than any other season of the Christian year.

I have written this study book as a simple resource to encourage a fuller reflection on the meaning and message of both seasons. Designed for group use, it is equally suited for personal devotion. The theme was not hard to decide upon; indeed, it leapt out at me the moment I sat down to write. The Bible is rich with promises that were either realised in the coming of Christ or that await their fulfilment in his coming again. In fact, there are so many that I soon found myself spoilt for choice. Initially, I intended to devote sessions to the great promises of the prophet Isaiah in chapters 9 and 11, but as the material developed it seemed more appropriate to focus on the key themes of Advent as traditionally observed: the return of Christ in judgement, the Word of God, the birth and role of John the Baptist, and the Annunciation. That covered the remit I started out with – namely, to prepare four sessions for

Advent – but it seemed only natural from there to move on to the Christmas message. In consequence, I have included material for the four weeks after Christmas, focusing in turn on Joseph's dream, the shepherds and Bethlehem, the journey of the magi, and, finally, the story of Anna and Simeon. The choice of the material is, of course, arbitrary, and you may feel that other promises would have been more appropriate. As I have already indicated, the range and number of biblical promises are almost endless, and if you can somehow weave more of these into the sessions – perhaps, for example, in the discussion times – so much the better. My aim has been simply to provide a framework through which to explore the rich promises of God associated with this time of year, and to ask what they continue to say to us today.

The format of this book is essentially the same as my Lent course, *Decisions, Decisions,* with just one significant addition. A selection of contemporary and traditional music that you may find helpful to aid meditation and reflection is suggested for each session (all available from Kevin Mayhew – see Appendix 3, page 79). The pieces can be used as an introduction or conclusion to the session, as aids to contemplation or as prayers in their own right. To encourage flexibility, I have purposely not accorded them a set place in each session.

The material in each study is set out as follows:

- Each begins with a traditional prayer, followed by a short paragraph introducing the overall theme.

- There then follows a short quiz (see Appendix 1, page 71). This is intended not only to help break the ice but also to encourage informal reflection on the issues covered in the study. Most of the questions are very simple, and should not take long to answer. Use this part of the session to encourage relaxed conversation and informality, but don't allow any discussion to continue for more than ten minutes at most. Time for a fuller discussion will come later. (Answers to each quiz can be found in Appendix 2, page 76.)

- Next comes a Bible passage (my own paraphrase). This should be read aloud by the group leader, or one of the group members. It may be worth checking that all participants are happy to read.
- The 'Comment' section that follows the reading is not intended for reading in a group context. Ideally, participants should study it before the meeting. Alternatively, allow a few minutes of quiet at this point, so that everyone can read and reflect on the issues raised.
- Run over the key points using the 'Summary' section and invite people's thoughts on the subject so far.
- Allow discussion to develop and introduce the suggested questions as and when appropriate.
- You may like to read the 'Further reading' passage at this point and weave this into the discussion. Alternatively, invite group members to reflect on this at home.
- After allowing ample time for discussion, use the meditation to draw people's thoughts together, and then, briefly, outline the suggestions for action. Invite any further ideas from among the group. The meditations from this book have been taken from my books *No Ordinary Man 2* and *To Put It Another Way* (Kevin Mayhew, 2000).
- Finally, end the meeting in prayer, using either the prayer provided or your own.

It is my hope that this series of studies will help us, individually or together, to recall some of the great promises associated with Advent and Christmas, and to make them our own.

NICK FAWCETT

Prayer

Loving God,
    we remember again your coming in Jesus Christ –
    your gift to humankind,
    your sharing our flesh and blood,
    your honouring of age-old promises
    spoken through the prophets.
We thank you for the reminder this time of year brings
    that you are a God we can depend on,
    one in whom we can put our trust, though all else fails.
So, we look forward in confidence
    to the ultimate fulfilment of your word –
    that day when Christ will be acclaimed
    as King of kings and Lord of lords.
Until then, we will trust in you,
    secure in your love,
    confident in your eternal purpose,
    assured that, in the fullness of time,
    your will shall be done.
Receive our thanks,
    in Jesus' name.
Amen.

First week of Advent

A disturbing promise

Prayer

Keep me, O Lord,
    while I tarry on this earth,
    in a daily serious seeking after thee
    and in a believing affectionate walking with thee;
    that when thou comest,
    I may be found not hiding my talent,
    nor yet asleep with my lamp unfurnished;
    but waiting and longing for my Lord,
    my glorious God,
    for ever and ever.
Amen.

Richard Baxter (1615-1691)

Introduction

How well are you able to cope with the unexpected? The answer, I suspect, depends on what the unexpected turns out to be. If you discover that you have won first prize in a competition, or inherited a fortune from a long-lost relative, then the chances are that you will respond rather well. On the other hand, should you return home after an evening out to discover a burst pipe, or arrive back at your car to discover you've been wheel-clamped for illegal parking, then you may not respond with quite so much relish. One other factor may also shape your response, and that is the sort of expectations you have in the first place. As an old saying puts it, 'Much of what we see depends on what we are looking for.'

    Our session today focuses on the Advent theme of expectation, asking both what we expect in terms of the return of Christ, and whether we are expecting the right thing. We begin in the Old

Testament, where the expectation of the Messiah was a recurring theme. It was this hope that sustained the Jewish nation through countless years of adversity. Yet, when Jesus came, only a handful of people were ready to receive him. Far from preparing people for his coming, expectation had the opposite effect. Why? Because the majority had made up their minds in advance as to the sort of Messiah God would send, and Jesus failed to match those expectations.

There is a danger that we today can make the same mistake. We may believe we are prepared for the return of Christ, ready to welcome him when he comes again, but our expectation may be a hindrance rather than help. Advent calls us to examine our pre-conceptions about the way God works, and to ask ourselves how open we are to God doing the unexpected in our lives.

Quiz

See Appendix 1, page 71.

Reading: Malachi 2:17-3:3a, 5

You have exhausted the Lord with all your talk, yet you ask, 'In what way have we wearied him?' By claiming that those who do evil are good in the sight of the Lord, and that he takes pleasure in them, and by asking, 'Where is the God of justice?' 'Look,' says the Lord of hosts, 'I am sending my messenger to prepare the way for me, so that the Lord whom you seek will suddenly come to his temple. The messenger of the covenant whom you so eagerly anticipate is coming, but who can endure the day of his coming or stand when he appears? For he is like a refiner's fire and fullers' soap; he will preside as a refiner and purifier of silver, and he will purify the descendants of Levi. I will approach you in judgement, and be swift to bear witness against the sorcerers, the adulterers and those who bear false witness; against those who exploit their hired workers, the widow and the orphan, who thrust aside the alien, and who do not fear me.'

Comment

One of the hit television shows of recent years has been *Blind Date*. Artificial and stage-managed it may be, but thousands of viewers nonetheless have delighted in the moment when a contestant's expectations are either fulfilled, exceeded or cruelly dashed as the moment of truth arrives and they meet the 'date' they have chosen face to face. For some it brings relief, for others, horror.

We may not personally have experienced a blind date, but we will all have made assumptions about people, many of which turned out to be completely unfounded. We assume, on first meeting someone, that we are going to get on like a house on fire, only to end up feeling awkward and tongue-tied. We imagine the learned intellectual will be aloof and reserved, and that the comedian will be the life and soul of the party, only to find the roles reversed. How many times, with the benefit of hindsight, have we ended up ruefully lamenting, 'They weren't quite what I expected'? The truth is our expectations are often flawed. The superstar, idolised by millions of fans across the world, proves to be as human as the next person, with just as many problems, foibles and weaknesses. The dream home we have struggled so hard to purchase turns out to have noisy neighbours, dry rot and planning permission for a dual carriageway at the bottom of the garden. The 'perfect couple' that we so much envied turn out to experience the same tensions, problems and stresses as we do. Expectations have a habit of being well wide of the mark.

It is precisely this danger of misplaced expectations that lies behind the words of the prophet Malachi. To those eagerly looking forward to the advent of the Messiah, he brought a stern, almost chilling warning that the day of the Lord would come upon them like a refiner's fire; a day to be feared rather than welcomed, for, far from bringing vindication after the long years of waiting, it would bring God's judgement and wrath. So what was the problem? How was it that the people's expectations could be so wide of the mark? Where had they gone wrong? The answer is very simple: they had put the future before the present, forgetting that the one

11

should influence the other – that their hope should change the way they lived, and the way they lived help to bring closer the fulfilment of their hope. Instead of working for the Messiah's kingdom, they were working against it: lying, cheating and deceiving; exploiting the poor and oppressing the weak. Their expectations of a glorious future age had led them to forget their responsibilities to God in the time and place where he had put them. Little wonder, then, that so many failed to recognise the Messiah when he came. They had become so preoccupied with the event of his coming that they had overlooked the sort of Messiah they should be expecting.

A sad mistake, we may say, but would we be so very different? The fact is that we can make a very similar mistake when it comes to a doctrine at the heart of Advent: the expectation of the second coming of Christ. For many that is a day when Jesus will return to put all the world's ills to right; a day when we, as Christians, will be translated into a glorious new kingdom. Yet, what does such language mean, and, more important, does it do justice to the biblical message as a whole? Undeniably, there are passages in both the Old Testament and the New that speak of the Son of Man returning as judge and king. Indeed, Jesus himself spoke in such terms. He also maintained, however, that the kingdom of heaven is within us. Similarly, John, in the fourth Gospel, emphasises that eternal life begins here and now.

The fact is, as Jesus warned the Apostles, that we don't know much about last times, nor do we need to know, for what should concern us is not the future but the present. What matters is how far our conviction that God's purpose will ultimately triumph shapes our daily lives – how far, in other words, we live by 'kingdom values', such as love, mercy, justice and peace. Pin all our hopes on some future time when we expect Jesus to come, and our very expectation may close our minds to what he is already doing among us. Worse, it may lead us to play down, or even overlook completely, our responsibility in working alongside him in the world today to help bring that kingdom closer.

One day, we believe, Jesus will come again to usher in a new age that will see the ultimate triumph of God's purposes. That hope is integral to Christian doctrine, but, when it comes to fleshing out what it means, the Bible is purposely long on imagery and short on detail, simply because we do not need to know when that time will be, how it will come or what it will be like. What matters is that we recognise that the second coming has implications for this and every day, for if we get that wrong the response we get from Jesus may be very different from the one we expected.

Summary

- Reality does not always correspond with our expectations; it may fall short or equally far exceed them.
- The Jews looked forward for centuries to the coming of the Messiah, but when Jesus came, the majority had no time for him.
- Our language concerning the second coming of Christ can lead us to abandon any hope or responsibility for this world, pinning our hopes instead on some future heavenly or earthly kingdom.
- While that future kingdom is an integral part of Christian belief, faith must also be about life now. Our conviction in God's sovereign purpose should make a difference in day-to-day life.
- Expectations can close our minds to other possibilities. We need to beware of allowing hope in the return of Christ to obscure the fact that he is already active in our world, and that he needs our involvement there too.

Discussion

- Are there ways in which you unconsciously dismiss this world, looking instead to a world to come?
- Is the faith you profess on Sunday evident in your life during the rest of the week?
- Are there things in your life you would be ashamed of were Jesus to return today? Isn't there a sense in which Jesus is present anyway? Why, then, act any differently now than you would do if you knew for certain that he would return tomorrow?

Further reading

Having come together, they asked him, 'Lord, is this the time when you are going to restore the kingdom to Israel?' He replied, 'It is not for you to know the times or seasons that the Father has decreed by his own authority, but you will receive power when the Holy Spirit has come upon you; and you will be my witnesses in Jerusalem, in all Judea and Samaria, and to the very ends of the earth.'

Acts 1:6-8

Meditation

The time is coming, they tell me:
    the day of the Lord's return,
    when we shall stand before him
    and he will separate the sheep from the goats,
    the wicked from the righteous –
So forget about the present,
    think instead of the future,
    for that's what matters –
    our final destiny,
    the life to come –
    nothing else.
Well, I'm sorry, but have I missed something?
For that's not the way I heard it,
    not what I thought Jesus was saying at all.
Keep alert, he warned, certainly,
    for the day will dawn as God has promised,
    but when that will be we've no idea;
    today, tomorrow or far beyond – who can say?
It's not the 'when' of his coming that should concern us,
    but the fact that he will,
    and the difference that makes
    not to the future but to the here and now,
    to the way we live every moment of every day.

We've a job to be doing,
      a broken world out there needing to hear
      his word and know his love,
      and that's what will concern him when he comes;
      not whether we've been looking forward eagerly
      to his kingdom
      but whether we're doing something to make it happen,
      to help build heaven on earth.
So what will he find in you?
A life dedicated to his service,
      continuing his ministry where he left off,
      or an obsession about the future so strong
      that you've forgotten about the present?
A life lived for others,
      committed to bringing light where there is darkness,
      and joy where there is sorrow,
      or a preoccupation with yourself,
      with securing your own salvation?
Don't think I doubt his promise.
The time is coming, just as they say,
      a day when we will be called to account,
      made to answer for the way we've lived our lives,
      but if I were you I wouldn't dwell on that too long,
      I'd get down to the business of discipleship,
      to walking the way of the cross,
      or otherwise you may find, when the moment comes
      and judgement is pronounced,
      that the verdict is very different from the one you had in mind.

Suggestions for action

- Identify some simple practical ways through which you can contribute to God's kingdom, and act upon them. Strive each moment to live more faithfully according to kingdom values. Live as though Christ *had* returned.

Prayer

Lord Jesus Christ
    you call us to be your body here on earth,
    to carry on the work you began during your earthly ministry,
    bringing hope and healing,
    light and love,
    to our bruised and battered world.
Forgive us for losing sight of that mission,
    for being so concerned with working out our own salvation
    that we forget what it really means;
    what is truly involved in Christian discipleship.
Teach us to anticipate your return
    by preparing the way for your coming;
    to catch a glimpse of your kingdom
    through living today by its values.
    Live in us now,
    so that the day may come
    when we live with you and all your people for all eternity;
    your will complete
    and your promise fulfilled.
In your name we ask it.
Amen.

Second week of Advent

A sure and certain promise

Prayer

Blessed Lord,
>who caused all holy Scriptures
>to be written for our learning:
>help us so to hear them,
>to read, mark, learn, and inwardly digest them
>that, through patience, and the comfort of your holy word,
>we may embrace and for ever hold fast
>the hope of everlasting life,
>which you have given us in our Saviour Jesus Christ.

Amen.

Alternative Service Book, Collect for Advent 2

Introduction

How many times have you gone back on your word to someone? Is there anybody who, hand on heart, can claim never to have broken a promise? I doubt it very much. It's not that we intend to – not usually anyway – more that circumstances alter, unforeseen eventualities arise, or we simply find ourselves unable to deliver on our pledge.

Advent reminds us of a different sort of word and different kind of promise – the Word made flesh and the promises of God. In Christ we see the fulfilment of God's age-old promises and the embodiment of his word throughout history, for he, like the Father, is before and beyond time. Human promises have a nasty habit of proving unreliable, however well-intentioned they may be. By contrast, what God says he will do, he does; his word is utterly dependable. Advent calls us to rejoice in the realisation of God's promise and to trust in all he has committed himself yet to do.

Quiz

See Appendix 1, page 72.

Reading: Isaiah 55:2-3, 10-11

Why spend your money on what is not bread? Why labour for what cannot satisfy? Listen instead to me, and you will eat richly, the best that anyone can offer. Come to me and listen to my words; give ear to what I am saying and you will have life. I will make a covenant with you, a covenant for all eternity, to love you as faithfully as I loved David. As the rain and snow come down from heaven and do not return until they have watered the earth – making it blossom and sprout, and giving seed to sow and bread for food – so it is with the word of my mouth; it will not return fruitless, but will accomplish my purpose and achieve that for which I sent it.

Comment

Have you written your Christmas cards yet? The chances are that you soon will, if you haven't already done so, but what exactly will you write? You may include a special message for those closest to you, perhaps share a little news with old friends and acquaintances, but for the majority your words will probably be something along the lines of 'With best wishes for Christmas and the New Year'. The words are well meant, sincere enough in their way, but we rarely translate them into anything more concrete. We promise to write again soon to that friend of yesteryear, but the chances are we will have no more contact with them until we send our cards again next Christmas. We fully intend to visit that church member no longer able to attend worship, but when Christmas is but a fading memory somehow we forget them too. We genuinely wish somebody the best of the season but fail to give them a second thought afterwards. Our words are so often only that – mere words.

At first sight, turning to the opening words of John's Gospel, you might be forgiven for thinking it's a case of the same old story, for here we find words about 'the Word'. 'In the beginning was the

Word, and the Word was with God, and the Word was God. He was in the beginning with God' (John 1:1-2). For John, this is where the Christmas story begins; not with the annunciation to Mary, or the stable at Bethlehem, or the announcement of the Saviour's birth to shepherds, but with God's word – the promises he had made to his people centuries earlier, and, before that, in the sovereign word spoken at the beginning of time. Imagine, though, if this was the end of the story; if all we had to go on, in terms of the Gospel, was God's word. How would we feel then? What cause would we have to celebrate? What news would we have to share? If everything were based only in words, what reason would any of us have to trust or believe? Yet, says John, God's word is a word with a difference, for, unlike our own, it is invariably backed up by actions, and will always ultimately be fulfilled. We see that the moment we open the Bible, there in the first chapter of Genesis:

> God said, 'Let there be light', and there was light. Then God said, 'Let the waters beneath the sky come together in one place, and let the dry land appear.' Again, it was so. After this, God said, 'Let the earth produce vegetation: plants yielding seed, and fruit trees of every conceivable kind, with seed-bearing fruit.' Once more, it was so.   *Genesis 1:3, 9, 11*

From the very beginning, God's word went hand in hand with action. What he said, he did; what he promised, he delivered; what he willed, he accomplished. With God, it was never a matter of good intentions or fine ideas; each time he spoke, things happened! A truth summed up in those wonderful words of the prophet Isaiah: '. . . so it is with the word of my mouth; it will not return fruitless, but will accomplish my purpose and achieve that for which I sent it.'

Isaiah was able to speak of God's purpose with conviction because he knew that when God says he will do something he does it! There could never be any question of God saying one thing and doing another, making a promise and then forgetting to honour it. He is a God who is wholly dependable, whose word will always be fulfilled; the God who declares: 'I am God, and

19

there is no other. I am God and there is none like me, pronouncing the end at the beginning and speaking at the dawn of time of things yet to be done, proclaiming, "My will shall prevail, and I will fulfil my purpose" . . . I have spoken, and I will make it happen; I have planned, and I will accomplish it.' (Isaiah 46:9, 11)

That, says John, sums up the true meaning of the birth of Christ; what Christmas is all about! It concerns what God has done; not just what he has said but what he has delivered on, not just what he promised but what he achieved! It speaks of the God who has acted decisively in human history, wonderfully and unmistakably putting his words into practice! 'The Word became flesh and lived among us, and we have seen his glory, the glory as of the Father's only Son, full of grace and truth' (John 1:14). God didn't just wish the world well and then leave it to get on with its own affairs. He didn't just tell us what we need to do and then expect us to struggle on as we best we can. He didn't give fine-sounding promises that remained only promises. He revealed love in action, the Word made flesh.

Here, then, is one of the great messages of Advent: that God's Word lived and breathed among us, sharing our humanity, walking our earth, matching words with deeds – the ultimate fulfilment of God's promise. It is a truth that speaks of the authenticity of all his promises; a reminder that God's word goes on being fulfilled each day, still having the power to challenge, inspire and change people's lives. We can trust that word like no other, knowing that it will not fail us; confident that what God has promised, he will do.

Summary

- Words can be cheap. Promises are easy to make but hard to honour. We say one thing but do another.
- At first sight, the opening words of John's gospel appear to be merely concerned with words.
- God's word, however, is different from our own, always accompanied by action and always ultimately fulfilled. It is utterly dependable and sure.

- The prophet Isaiah reminds us of the active nature of God's word, constantly at work until it has achieved its purpose.
- We see the ultimate fulfilment of God's word in the coming of Christ, the Word made flesh.
- The Incarnation reminds of the trustworthiness of all God's promises, and of the word that continues to change lives and shape the world today.

Discussion

- Why do we find promises so hard to keep? What things prevent you honouring your promises?
- What promises of God have you found most helpful in your life? Which promises have you personally found fulfilled?
- Which promises concerning the future mean most to you?

Further reading: 2 Corinthians 1:17-20

Do I make my plans according to ordinary human standards, ready to say 'Yes, yes' and 'No, no' at the same time? As surely as God is faithful, our word to you has not been 'Yes and No';...but in him it is always 'Yes'. For in him every one of God's promises is a 'Yes'. For this reason it is through him that we say the 'Amen', to the glory of God.

Meditation

'Where did it all start?' they ask me.
'Tell us the story again.'
And I know just what they want to hear –
    about the inn and the stable,
    the baby lying in a manger,
    shepherds out in the fields by night,
    and wise men travelling from afar.

21

I know why they ask, of course I do,
    for which of us hasn't thrilled to those marvellous events,
    that astonishing day when the Word became flesh,
    dwelling here on earth amongst us?
Yet wonderful though that all is, it's not where it started,
    and if we stop there,
    then we see only a fraction of the picture,
    the merest glimpse
    of everything God has done for us in Christ.
We have got to go right back to see more –
    before Bethlehem,
    before the prophets,
    before the Law,
    before time itself, would you believe? –
    for that's where it started:
    literally 'In the beginning'.
Yes, even there the saving purpose of God was at work,
    his creating, redeeming word bringing light and love
    into the world,
    shaping not just the heavens and the earth but the lives of all,
    every man, woman and child.
That's the mind-boggling wonder of it –
    the fact not just that God made us,
    but that through Christ he was determined from the outset
    to share our lives,
    to take on our flesh,
    to identify himself totally with the joys and sorrows,
    the beauty and the ugliness, of humankind.
It defies belief, doesn't it?
Yet it's true –
    God wanting us to know him not as his creatures
    but as his children,
    not as puppets forced to dance to his tune
    but as people responding freely to his love,
    and to do that he patiently and painstakingly prepared the way,
    revealing year after year a little more of his purpose,

a glimpse more of his kingdom,
until at last, in the fullness of time,
the Word became flesh and lived among us;
full of grace and truth.
It wasn't an afterthought, the incarnation,
a last-ditch attempt to make the best of a bad job –
it was planned from the dawn of time.
So next time you hear the story of the stable and the manger,
of the shepherds gazing in wonder
and the magi kneeling in homage,
stop for a moment and reflect on everything
that made it all possible,
the eternal purpose that so carefully prepared
the way of Christ,
and then rejoice that this same purpose
embraces not simply others,
but includes you!

Suggestions for action

- Build in a little time each day to read the Bible. Don't make this a matter of routine or duty, but approach it in a spirit of dialogue, bringing your joys, sorrows, faith and doubt before God and asking what he may be saying to you through his word.

- Ask yourself, honestly, how far you have trusted in God's promises, and, equally, how far you have honoured your promises to him.

- Resolve to honour a promise that you have made to someone but failed to keep. Take the first steps today in putting the situation right.

Prayer

Sovereign God,
we thank you that you are a God on whom we can depend;
a God in whom we can put our trust.
What you promise, you do;
what you purpose, you accomplish.

We remember your promise to Abraham
    that, through his offspring, all the world would be blessed;
    to Moses, that you would lead the Israelites out of Egypt;
    to Isaiah, that you would deliver your people from exile;
    to your prophets, that the Messiah would come;
    to the Apostles, that he would rise again on the third day.
We thank you that you fulfilled those promises,
    just as you said you would –
    your Son born from the line of Abraham;
    your chosen nation set free from slavery;
    your people returning joyfully to Jerusalem,
    your promised deliverer, born in Bethlehem;
    your power seen in the resurrection of Christ.
We thank you for what that means for us today –
    that we can live each moment with confidence,
    whatever our circumstances may be,
    whatever times of testing may befall us,
    knowing that, though all else may fail,
    you will not;
    though heaven and earth may pass away,
    your words will endure for ever.
So we look forward to that day when your purpose is fulfilled
    and you are all in all,
    and, until then, we will trust in you,
    secure in your love, confident in your eternal purpose,
    assured that your will shall be done.
Receive our thanks, in the name of Christ.
Amen.

Third week of Advent

An incredible promise

Prayer

Merciful God,
   you have prepared for those who love you
   such good things as pass human understanding.
Pour into our hearts such love towards you
   that we, loving you above all things,
   may obtain your promises
   which exceed all that we can desire
   through Jesus Christ our Lord.
Amen.

from The Daily Office

Introduction

Some promises take a bit of believing, don't they? I should know, for I've made more than a few such promises myself. As I write these words, the manuscript for my next book should have been finished over two months ago, whereas in fact it is only three quarters finished. I pledged to write four books over the course of the year, but already that is starting to look hopelessly optimistic. I could have done it, had everything gone to plan. Had I not needed to earn a living in the meantime, and had the editing contracts I took on not turned out to be so complicated, I could probably have finished, maybe even written more books than promised rather than less. The problem is that life doesn't run smoothly. We live in the real world, not an ideal universe; a world that puts all kinds of unforeseen constraints upon us. When I prepare my writing schedule for next year, it will probably be taken with a firm pinch of salt; the inevitable suspicion that I may again have promised more than I can deliver.

Though we'd never admit it, we can feel a similar sense of scepticism when it comes to the promises of God. We talk about his life-changing power – his ability to transform people and situations in ways that defy understanding – but we find it ever harder to believe. More alarming still, we fail even to consider the possibility that God is able to overturn our expectations. Our experience of broken promises, and our failure even to live up to our own, rubs off on our faith; God is tarred with the same brush as everyone else. It can't be done, we tell ourselves; such things no longer happen, not in the world as we know it. Advent – and, in particular, the story of Elizabeth and Zechariah – reminds us that though some things are beyond *us*, nothing is beyond God!

Quiz
See Appendix 1, page 72.

Reading: Luke 1:5-20
In the days of King Herod of Judea, there was a certain priest named Zechariah, who belonged to the priestly order of Abijah, whose wife, called Elizabeth, was a descendant of Aaron. Both were righteous before God, scrupulously following the commandments and ordinances of the Lord. However, they had no children, Elizabeth being infertile, and both were getting on in years.

It so happened that, while he was performing his priestly duties before God as part of his section, the lot that was customarily made among the priesthood fell on to him to enter the inner sanctuary of the Lord and to offer incense there, during which time the gathered assembly of the people prayed outside. Suddenly, an angel of the Lord appeared to him, standing on the right-hand side of the altar of incense. On seeing him, Zechariah was awestruck and paralysed by fear, but the angel said to him, 'Do not be afraid, Zechariah, for your plea has been heard. Your wife Elizabeth will bear you a son, and you are to call him John. He will bring you joy and gladness, and many will rejoice at his birth, for he will be great in the eyes of the Lord. He must never drink wine or strong drink; even while he is in the womb he will be filled with the Holy Spirit. He will turn many of the people of Israel to the Lord their God, and he will go out in the spirit and power of Elijah to turn the hearts of parents to their children, and the disobedient to the wisdom of the righteous – to prepare people so that they are ready for the Lord.' Zechariah said to the angel, 'How can I know this is true? For I am an old man, and my wife also is getting on in years.' The angel replied, 'I am Gabriel. I stand in God's presence, and he has sent me to tell you this good news, but now, since you have not believed my words that in due course will be fulfilled, you will be struck dumb, rendered mute until the day these things happen.'

Comment

A short while ago, a group of scientists triumphantly announced an astonishing breakthrough – after years of painstaking research, they had successfully unravelled the human genome, the genetic blueprint that determines our physical make-up. Their discovery had one thing in common with a long tradition of scientific discovery and, indeed, with the achievements of those in our quiz earlier – the project they embarked on was initially considered by many to be impossible. 'It can't be done,' they chorused, before the Wright brothers made the first successful powered flight. 'It's impossible!' they said, when it was first suggested that a rocket might land on the moon. 'You must be out of your mind!' Yet, each time, the sceptics were proved wrong; what had seemed to be out of the question was shown to be anything but.

It's easy, with the benefit of hindsight, to condemn such doubters for their lack of faith, but which of us would have been different in their shoes? Faced by a claim that runs contrary to all received wisdom, it is only natural to err on the side of caution, if not disbelief. We should not be surprised, then, by the response of Zechariah to the news that his wife Elizabeth was to give birth to a son. Whether Elizabeth was strictly beyond childbearing years we are not told, but it is clear than any hopes the couple might have had of her conceiving were long since dead and buried. They were reconciled to their disappointment, determined to face the facts, however painful those might be; so suddenly to be told that a child was to be born to them after all must have been hard to swallow – almost, you might say, too good to be true. Again, would we have responded any differently? I don't think so. Remember, just a few months later, Mary was to express similar doubts at another heavenly promise, albeit that her reservations were for somewhat different reasons. 'How can this be,' she asked, 'since I am a virgin?'

It is worth pushing the analogy between these two stories further, for the lesson is the same in both, summed up in one simple statement: 'With God nothing is impossible.' That is what Mary was to discover following her initial doubts, and that is what Zechariah was to discover in turn. Make no mistake, there was nothing misguided about their reactions at a human level. On the contrary, both responses represented sound common sense. The promises made to them were preposterous, unthinkable, out of this world – but that was the whole point. They were dealing not with human promises but the will of God – the God who defies human understanding, whose ways are beyond us, who dictates what *shall be* instead of being ruled by what *is!* Here is the God who parted the waters of the Red Sea, who fed his people with manna from heaven, who demolished the walls of Jericho and who equipped David to overcome Goliath; the God who, in Christ, stilled the storm, healed the sick and rose from the tomb. Humanly speaking, there was no way such things could be done, each situation seeming beyond redemption, but with God it was a different story, all things possible for him.

For us today, there will be times when we find God's promises hard to accept for all kinds of reasons. Can he possibly change our lives, despite all our doubts and weaknesses? It seems impossible. Can he really make a difference to this world of ours, racked by so much hatred, bitterness, corruption and selfishness? Again, it seems impossible. Can he truly love us if he allows so much pain and suffering, so much that seems to contradict his will? Yet again, it seems impossible. Can there conceivably be life after death, hope beyond the grave; and, if so, where will it be, what will it be like and when will it happen? It just seems too good to believe. There's nothing wrong with asking such questions; indeed, it's perfectly natural that we should, for there is so much in life that seems to deny any prospect of God's promises being realised. Much as we want to accept them, reason stands in the way. Yet there are times when we must go beyond reason and take the leap of faith – not a blind leap into the unknown but a measured response based on the experience of those who have gone before us and, despite their initial doubts, have learned beyond question that truly nothing is impossible with God.

Summary

- It is natural to greet stupendous claims with scepticism, if not disbelief, yet what seems impossible is finally often achieved.
- If that is true in terms of human ingenuity and accomplishment, then it is all the more so when it comes to God.
- After years of disappointment, Zechariah understandably found it hard to believe that his wife would conceive, but such a response was to reckon without God.
- Across the years, God has repeatedly achieved that which the world deems impossible, his ways beyond our ways and his power greater than anything we can comprehend.
- Many of God's promises may seem hard to accept, however much we want to believe them. We need, sometimes, to look beyond the narrow confines of human reason and learn that with God nothing is impossible!

Discussion

- Are there ways in which God has overturned your expectations, helping you or those known to you to achieve what seemed impossible?

- Which promises of God do you find it hardest to believe? Do events such as the demolition of the Berlin Wall and the end of apartheid help you to believe that what seemed impossible can be achieved?
- What is the difference between 'blind' faith and informed trust? How can we know the difference?
- Which are you: the sort of person who says, 'It can't be done' or the sort who says, 'It can!'?

Further reading: Philippians 3:20

Now to the one who, through his sovereign power, is able to do incalculably more than we can begin to ask or even think of, to him be glory in the Church and in Christ Jesus in this and every generation. Amen.

Meditation

I wanted to believe it, honestly!
After all those years trying,
    all those false hopes and crushing disappointments,
    there was nothing I wanted to believe more.
A child!
A son!
At our time of life!
Wonderful!
But that was the trouble –
    we were too old,
    not just over the hill but well down the other side,
    and we'd both accepted we just weren't meant to be parents.
It hurt, of course it did,
    but little by little we'd come to terms,
    the pain easing as we threw ourselves into what was left us.
So why suddenly this strange vision,
    this sense of God speaking to me in a way so real and powerful
    it was as though an angel was there in person,
    spelling out the message word for word?

To be frank, I felt we could do without it, both of us,
    and, whatever else, there was no way I intended
    to go running back to Elizabeth
    opening up old wounds.
So I just laughed it off,
    shrugged my shoulders and carried on
    as though nothing had happened.
Let's face it, I reasoned, a few more years
    and we'd be pushing up the daisies,
    an end to life's mysteries once and for all.
Well, I couldn't have been more wrong, could I?
For it happened,
    every last word of it,
    down to the final detail!
How did I feel?
Well, you can imagine.
Ecstatic!
Just about beside myself with joy!
It was the proudest and most wonderful moment of my life,
    and for a time after the birth I could think of nothing else,
    every moment too precious to waste.
Yet, I've been thinking recently about those words
    spoken by the angel,
    for when he spoke of John's coming,
    he talked also of the role he was destined to fulfil:
    'He will turn many of the people of Israel to the Lord their God.
    With the spirit and power of Elijah he will go before him,
    to make ready a people prepared for the Lord.'
I forgot that afterwards in all the excitement,
    too much else going on to give it a second thought.
But do you think it could possibly mean what I think it does?
God's promised Messiah, coming at last.
A child, born to me, that was wonderful!
But for us all,
    a child to change the world –
    could that really be?

Suggestions for action

- Remind yourself of those promises God has fulfilled, both during the course of history and in your own life.
- Reflect further on God's promises concerning the future and ask yourself what they mean to you.
- If God has been challenging you to do something that you feel to be beyond you, ask yourself if now is the time to respond. Stop allowing your own limited horizons to obscure what God is able to do.

Prayer

Loving God,
  for all our faith there are some things we consider beyond us
  and beyond you.
Belief says one thing but realism another,
  and in consequence we set limits
  to the way you are able to work in our lives.
Yet, time and again you have overturned human expectations,
  demonstrating that all things are possible for those who love you.
Teach us, then, to look beyond the obvious and immediate,
  and to live rather in the light of your sovereign grace
  through which you are able to do far more
  than we can ever ask or imagine.
Through Jesus Christ our Lord.
Amen.

Fourth week of Advent

A demanding promise

Prayer

Teach me, good Lord,
> to serve you as you deserve;
> to give, and not to count the cost;
> to fight, and not to heed the wounds;
> to toil, and not to seek for rest;
> to labour, and not to ask for any reward,
> save that of knowing that I do your will,
> through Jesus Christ my Lord.

Amen.

Prayer of St Ignatius Loyola

Introduction

You don't get something for nothing, we are often told, and as life goes by we learn how true that is. Any offer that promises us gifts for free usually has a catch somewhere, it being necessary to put something in before we can get something out.

The same is true of Christianity, despite the impression often given. We talk loosely, sometimes, about the gift of new life freely offered to all in Christ, as though it requires no input on our part. Strictly speaking, we are right, in that we cannot earn such a gift; we simply receive it through grace – yet that risks giving a highly misleading picture, for genuine commitment to Christ necessarily involves a response. Throughout the gospels, Jesus repeatedly talks of the cost of discipleship and the price of following him, even suggesting that the sincerity of our faith will be measured by our willingness to act upon it. God's goodness may be freely given, but it nonetheless makes demands upon us. Nowhere is that better illustrated than in the Annunciation – an encounter with God that simultaneously involved a glorious promise alongside the most daunting of challenges.

Quiz
See Appendix 1, page 73.

Reading: Luke 1:26-35, 38

Now in the sixth month the angel Gabriel was sent by God to a town in Galilee called Nazareth, to a virgin engaged to a man named Joseph, a member of the house of David. The virgin's name was Mary. Approaching her, he said, 'Greetings, you who have been highly favoured. The Lord is with you.' She was bewildered by his words, and contemplated what such a greeting might mean. The angel said to her, 'Don't be frightened, Mary, for you have found favour with God, for you will conceive in your womb and bear a son, and you will give him the name "Jesus". He will be great, and will be called the Son of the Most High, and the Lord God will give him the throne of his ancestor David. He will reign over the house of Jacob for ever, and his kingdom will never end.' Mary said to the angel, 'How can this be, since I am a virgin?' The angel answered, 'The Holy Spirit will come upon you, and the power of the Most High will rest over you, so that the child you will bear will be called the Son of God . . . for with God nothing is impossible.' Mary responded, 'I am the Lord's servant. Let it be to me just as you say.'

Comment

If someone were to ask a favour of you, how would you respond? The answer, of course, would depend on what was being asked. If it involved only a couple of minutes of your time, no real effort or inconvenience on your part, then you would probably be only too happy to oblige. If, on the other hand, it meant sacrificing weeks, months, or even perhaps a lifetime of commitment, you might understandably think twice. More than likely, you'd come up with some reason why, much though you'd like to help, there is no way you can do so, and, failing that, you might grudgingly agree in the vain hope that something might turn up to get you off the hook. All of which makes the response of Mary to the message of Gabriel so astonishing and challenging, because the 'favour' God asked of her could hardly have been more demanding. 'You will conceive in your womb and bear a son.' (Luke 1:31)

Was God, however, actually asking something from Mary? On first reading, it may not look like it. Indeed, according to Gabriel, the favour was the other way round: Mary had *found favour* with God and been singled out for the honour of bearing his son. Yet, standing where she was, it must have seemed very different. Had she been married, it might have been another story. Had she been itching to start a family, it could conceivably have been the best news in world. So far as we know, however, she had no desire for children just then, and she most certainly wasn't married, so the news that she would imminently bear a child must have been just about the last thing she wanted to hear. Think about it from her point of view. One moment she was happily betrothed; the next, asked to surrender her very body to God. One moment her future seemed sure; the next her life was turned upside down, never to be the same again. One moment she hadn't a care in the world; the next she was being asked to bear the opprobrium of society – to jeopardise her marriage, her good name and her long-term security.

So what did she say? 'Not on your life'? 'Think again, Lord'? 'Are you serious'? Any such response would have been hugely understandable. But, no! Instead: 'I am the Lord's servant. Let it be to me just as you say' (Luke 1:38). Is it any wonder that, in some quarters of the Church, Mary has been revered ever since? Where others would have run a mile, Mary responded in faith. Where most would have vehemently protested, Mary accepted God's will. Hers was a truly astonishing example of faith and trust, through which God was able to work to fulfil his promise of a Messiah. Mary understood – as apostles, martyrs, preachers, teachers and ordinary everyday disciples came to understand after her – that God's promise involves giving as well as receiving, cost as well as reward, responsibility as well as privilege.

Thank goodness, God doesn't ask anything so demanding from any of us, we might say, but if we think that we are making a big mistake. To read this passage as though it is concerned simply with a special person long ago is to misunderstand the way God works and the challenge he continues to bring. It's as much about you and me today, because God needs to use us just as he used Mary. If some promises have been resolved, others still await their fulfilment, and we have to help make that happen. Think of the words of Isaiah in chapter 9 concerning the people who walked in darkness seeing a great light, or in chapter 11 concerning a new era in which all will live in harmony together. Can we sit back and leave the fulfilment of such prophecies to God? Can we disown this world and postpone the realisation of such a vision to the day when God's kingdom is finally established? Of course not! The final victory may be then, but the spadework begins now. God needs our witness and service, our willingness to spread light in the darkness and hope in the wilderness, our resolve to express his love through word and deed. He wants to come *to* us in Christ so that he can come *through* us to others, and to do either he needs our willingness to say along with Mary: 'I am the Lord's servant. Let it be to me just as you say.'

Summary

- Few of us are ready to put ourselves out for anyone.
- Mary was asked to put herself out for God. His promise to her involved a costly response on her part. The fulfilment of his promise to the world depended on her willingness to bear that cost.
- Mary was ready to let God overturn her life and use her as he saw fit. Do we have the same faith and commitment?
- We, in turn, have a vital part to play in the realisation of God's promises. He needs our response, just as he needed that of Mary.

Discussion

- In some parts of the world, discipleship can still be costly, involving persecution, loss of freedom or even death. Is there any sense in which it can be costly for us too?
- Are there times when you have backed away from God's call, for fear of the consequences?
- Do you take seriously the demanding nature of discipleship? Is there a danger of overstressing your personal relationship with Christ at the cost of your responsibilities in working towards the growth of his kingdom?
- Why do you think it is that the Church tends to be stronger in places where being a Christian involves repression and danger than in countries where individuals are free to worship as they will?

Further reading: Luke 9:23-24

He said to all, 'If any want to come after me, let them deny themselves and take up their cross daily, and then follow me. For those wishing to save their life will lose it, but those who lose their life for my sake will save it.'

Meditation

'You've got it wrong! ' I told him.
'You can't mean me,
    no way!
Someone else perhaps,
    more worthy,
    more important,
    but not me!'
Honestly, what did I have to commend me?
No connections or special qualities,
    nothing –
    just an ordinary girl from Nazareth –
    so what could God see in me?

But it was academic anyway, for I wasn't even married yet,
    and there was no way I'd sleep with Joseph until I was.
So I came out with it straight,
    'Sorry, but you're wrong!'
Only he wouldn't take no for an answer.
Just stood there smiling,
    unruffled;
    and before I knew it he was off again –
    the message even more fantastic than before –
    God's power overshadowing me,
    a child born of the Holy Spirit,
    the Son of God!
It was way over the top,
    and I should have turned him out there and then,
    but I was flummoxed,
    too amazed to reply.
Even when I found my tongue it wasn't much use to me –
    can you believe it, my mind brimming over with questions
    and what did I say? –
    'Here am I, the servant of the Lord,
    let it be to me according to your word.'
Oh, it sounded good, granted –
    the epitome of humility –
    but if you only knew what I was thinking,
    you'd have a different picture then.
So what got into me, you ask?
How could I be so meek and accepting?
Well, what choice did I have, let's be honest,
    for as the angel said, 'With God, nothing will be impossible.'
How could I argue with that?
There was no way out, was there?
But it's one thing to accept that in principle,
    another when it turns your life upside down.
Do I believe it?
Well, I didn't at the time,
    but I do now,
    for I've just discovered I'm pregnant,

and I say this perfectly reverently, God knows how!
It's astonishing and terrifying,
    exciting yet mystifying,
    my mind in turmoil, not quite sure what to think any more.
But one thing is plain now,
    beyond all question –
    with him, quite clearly, nothing *is* impossible!

Suggestions for action

- Put your faith into practice this week. Instead of talking about love, express it in action. Instead of planning to witness to Christ, share your faith with someone.
- Next time you receive an appeal from a charity asking for money, don't just screw it up and throw it away. Deny yourself something you were planning to buy and give the money away instead.
- Next time a request is put out in your church for helpers, volunteers or someone to take on a position of responsibility, don't just look at the wall and hope no one picks on you. Ask yourself if you fit the bill and, if so, be ready to play your part.

Prayer

Gracious God,
    you may not ask of us what you asked of Mary,
    but nonetheless your challenge comes to each one of us,
    calling us to avenues of service
    which we would never imagine possible.
Whoever we are, we all have a part to play in your purposes,
    a unique role in making real the love of Christ
    here on earth, here and now.
Grant us the humility we need to hear your voice
    and the faith we need to respond.
Like Mary, let us be ready to answer when you call:
    'I am the Lord's servant. Let it be to me just as you say.'
In Jesus' name.
Amen.

First week after Christmas

A personal promise

Prayer

Merciful God,
    you have prepared for those who love you
    such good things as pass human understanding.
Pour into our hearts such love towards you
    that we, loving you above all things,
    may obtain your promises
    which exceed all that we can desire
    through Jesus Christ our Lord.
Amen.

from The Daily Office

Introduction

Do you remember the advertising campaign that preceded the launch of the National Lottery? It caused quite a controversy at the time: a giant hand hovering over the rooftops of a town before finally a finger stretched out to single out one household as the lucky winner of the coveted jackpot, backed up by the words, 'It could be you!' The suggestion was that the hand of providence might one day select us to receive a fortune. Did you take the bait? Many have, and a number of people have become millionaires as a result, but the majority of participants will have spent a considerable amount of money with little if anything to show for it.

Contrast that with the events of Bethlehem that we are once again celebrating now. Here was the promise of riches, not on earth but in heaven; a prize not merely for this life but for all eternity; the greatest gift ever offered. Yet, this was no lottery, dependent on the whim of fate. There was no question of it _could_ be you if you happen to get lucky. The message of the angels, the evangelists and countless generations of faith since is, quite simply, 'It *is* you!' The promise of God in Christ – his gift of new life with everything that means – is not reserved for the exclusive few, nor dependent on any quirk of chance. It is yours for the taking, waiting simply for you personally to claim it – for you, for me, for everyone!

Quiz

See Appendix 1, page 73.

Reading: Matthew 1:18-25

Now the birth of Jesus Christ started like this. When his mother Mary had become engaged to Joseph, but before they lived together, she was found to be pregnant, through the work of the Holy Spirit. Joseph, being a fair man and not wanting to publicly humiliate her, resolved quietly to dismiss her. Just as he was deciding this, however, an angel of the Lord appeared to him in a dream and said, 'Joseph, son of David, do not be afraid to take Mary as your wife, for the child she carries is conceived by the Holy Spirit. She will bear a son, and you are to call him Jesus, for he will save his people from their sins.' All this occurred to fulfil the Lord's word spoken through the prophet: 'See, the virgin will conceive and bear a son, and they will call him Emmanuel', which means, 'God is with us'. When Joseph awoke from sleep, he did as the angel of the Lord had instructed: he took her as his wife, but had no sexual relations with her until she had borne a son; and he named him Jesus.

Comment

If you were sending out an invitation to advertise some event you were planning or to interest people in a project, what format would you use? A glossy pamphlet, perhaps, or a printed card, or would you opt instead for a simple letter giving details of the place, time and so on? I ask, because an article caught my eye recently, discussing the relative effectiveness of the various written approaches made to students and young people during the so-called Decade of Evangelism. Bottom of the list by a long way was the impersonal mailshot. You know the sort of thing – a bit like the double-glazing sales literature or the like that drops through our door with such depressing regularity. Almost as unattractive was a standard circular with the recipient's name filled in at the top, to give some semblance of the personal touch. Interestingly, there wasn't even much interest in a genuinely personal letter that had been produced on a word processor, presumably because it still carried formal overtones. What most effectively captured people's attention and made them want to read on was a handwritten envelope with a handwritten letter inside.

Why? The answer, I suspect, is quite simply that you can't beat the personal touch. Here was a letter addressed to them and written to them; a letter that showed someone cared enough about them personally to take the time to write. It may not guarantee success, but it is more likely to cut ice than any other approach. This perhaps goes some way to explaining not only the enduring power of the Christmas message but also the continuing ability of the gospel to speak to generations the world over, for it is this approach that lies at the heart of both.

There is a sense in which God had tried the more formal approach, having spoken through the Law, prophets, judges and kings, but with the coming of Christ he revealed his love in an altogether more compelling way. As the writer to the Hebrews put it, 'In times past, God spoke in various ways by his prophets to our ancestors, but in these last days he has spoken to us by a Son' (1:1-2). What was needed, and what God gave, was the personal touch: the Word made flesh, sharing our humanity, walking our earth, experiencing our hopes and fears, joys and sorrows. Here is the God who came to Mary and Joseph, to shepherds out in the fields, to wise men in the East, to the crowds that flocked to hear Jesus; the God who, most important of all, continues to come personally to us today. A truth summed up in those unforgettable words to Joseph, 'They shall name him Emmanuel', which means

'God is with us'. Not, God *may* be with us, nor God *was* with us, nor even God *will* be with us, but God *is* with us. Equally important, it was not God is with *some*, or God is with *them*, but God is with *us*!

This is the wonderful message of Christmas and the glorious truth at the heart of the gospel: that each one of us can know God personally, and not just at some distant point in the future or in some distant heavenly realm but here and now, in the routine business of everyday life! Here is what this season is all about: not just a celebration of the Christ who came, but a joyful welcoming of the Christ who comes; a glad and personal response to the Christ whom we can know for ourselves, who accepts us as ourselves and who wants us truly to be ourselves. It is a message that has spoken to generations across the centuries, but above all it is God's message today to *you*!

Summary

- People respond more to the personal touch than to any amount of impersonal glossy hype.
- The heart of Christmas and the gospel message is that God took on human flesh in Christ, so that each one of us can know him in person.
- Christmas is not simply about the past and the story of others; it is about today and about you, inviting you to share in a personal relationship with God.

Discussion

- What do you understand by a personal relationship with God? How is it possible to know Christ? In what ways do you experience his presence in your own life?
- Are there ways in which you still see the gospel or the promises of God as being about others rather than yourself?
- How would you sum up the gift of God in Christ? What aspects are most important to you personally?

Further reading: John 1:13-14

To as many as received him and who believed in his name, he
gave the right to become children of God; children born not of
blood or any union of the flesh, nor of any human desire, but of
God.

Meditation

It was the strangest of dreams,
    ludicrous really,
      yet I just can't get it out of my mind.
You see, I dreamt God was speaking to me.
No, not face to face, I don't mean that,
    but through this angel, claiming to be his special messenger.
And do you know what he told me?
Take Mary to be your wife, that's what.
Just when I'd decided to put her quietly aside,
    hush up the scandal as best I could,
    this character telling me to think again.
And why?
Because apparently it was nothing to do with her,
    the baby she's carrying not the result of some fleeting passion,
    but conceived of the Holy Spirit,
    ordained by God himself.
Well, I've heard some excuses in my time
    but that one really takes the biscuit!
I mean, who did the fellow think I was –
    some fool born yesterday?
It was laughable,
    and I'd usually have dismissed it without a second thought.
Yet I didn't –
    not then,
    not now.
A dream it may have been,
    but it's lived with me,
    as vivid today as when I first dreamt it.

I can't say why exactly –
    it was a mixture of things I suppose.
There was Mary for a start,
    the way she looked at me as she broke the news –
    so trusting,
    so innocent,
    almost as though she too had met with God
    and was confident I would understand.
Then there was Elizabeth and Zechariah –
    heaven knows what got into them,
    but they were simply delighted,
    no hint of suspicion, let alone scandal, as far as they saw it –
    I suppose that boy of theirs, after so many disappointments,
    was enough to turn anyone's mind.
But what really swung it was this feeling deep within
    that somehow God had touched me;
    that, like it or not, life was changed for ever.
I was right in that, wasn't I?
    for we're on the road to Bethlehem as I speak,
    my wife heavy with child,
    wincing with pain,
    praying it's not much further.
Did I do right, standing by her?
I still have my doubts, even now,
    still find it hard to meet her eye,
    for it takes some getting used to, a child you had no part in –
    but, despite the questions, I've done my best for her,
    taking her for my wife, just as I was told.
Now it's God's turn, isn't it? –
    over to him for the Saviour to be born,
    God with us!
Was it a dream, a figment of my imagination?
We'll soon see, won't we?

Suggestions for action

- Ask yourself whether faith is still about a personal relationship with Christ or whether it has become a matter of routine or duty.
- Acknowledge the state of your faith openly and honestly before God, and ask him to break through the barriers that have come between you and him.
- Consciously devote more time each day to quiet devotion and reflection, allowing God to speak to you in Christ.

Prayer

Loving God,
    you have given all the world good news in Christ.
Help us to hear that news afresh each day,
    recognising it as good news for us, here and now.
Help us to receive it with both our minds and our hearts,
    always looking to understand more of what it continues to say;
    and help us to share what Christ has done for *us*,
    so that others in turn may celebrate what he has done for *them*.
In his name, we ask it.
Amen.

Second week after Christmas

A surprising promise

Prayer

O God the Eternal,
>the refuge and help of all your children,
>in our weakness you are our strength,
>in our darkness you are our light,
>in our sorrow you are our comfort and peace.

We cannot number your blessings.
We cannot declare your love.
For all your goodness we bless you.
May we ever live as in your presence
>and love the things you love
>and serve you with the service of our daily lives.

Through Jesus Christ our Lord.
Amen.

Prayer of St Boniface

Introduction

I was invited to a special event recently – the annual Christian Booksellers' Convention, held this year in Doncaster. Like most big events, it had an impressive line-up of Christian celebrities: Stephen Gaukroger and Graham Kendrick to name but two. I was highly honoured to be among the supporting cast, this being my first (and probably last!) time moving among such exalted company. No self-respecting showpiece occasion would be without their quota of big names: a Cliff Richard, Steve Chalke or Nicky Gumbel to top the bill. These are the sort of people who will pull in the crowds, make an impression, create a stir, and of course there's nothing wrong with that. We see something similar in most secular events. A member of the royal family is asked to open a new public building; a film or pop star is engaged to promote a new product; a local event boasts the town's mayor or the constituency MP as guest of honour; and so it continues.

One event, though, was different: the birth of Jesus. Here was the single most important moment in history, an occasion that the people of God had longed for over countless centuries – God at last coming to redeem his people. So whom did he invite as his special guests? Who were the first to hear and see the good news? The answer, of course, is shepherds – ordinary people like you and me, going about their ordinary business and no doubt expecting just another ordinary day. Yet they, like so many others, were to discover that God is able to use what seems ordinary in the most extraordinary of ways.

Quiz

See Appendix 1, page 74.

Reading: Micah 5:2-5a

From you, Bethlehem of Ephrathah, small though you may be among the clans of Judah, shall emerge one who is to rule in Israel, whose roots go back into history, from the earliest of times. Therefore, he will give up his people only until the time when she who is in labour bears a child; then the remnant of his people will return to their kinsfolk in Israel. He will stand and feed his flock in the strength of the Lord, in the majesty of the name of the Lord his God. Thus, they will live in safety, for at that time his greatness will extend to the ends of the earth; and he will be the one of peace.

Comment

If you were to set yourself the target of writing a blockbuster book destined to shoot straight to the top of the bestseller list and earn you sufficient royalties to live in comfort for rest of your life, what sort of theme would you choose for your story? The range of story-lines is potentially endless, but you could do a lot worse than write a rags-to-riches novel. You know the sort of thing – the tale of someone who rises from obscure and humble beginnings to achieve greatness, starting out with absolutely nothing yet battling against the odds to carve out unprecedented success. Yes, I know it's been done countless times before and that it all sounds a little corny, yet innumerable variations on this theme have captured the imagination of generations across the years – the stuff not only of fairy stories, but of films, dramas, soap operas, legend and folklore. What is the secret of its appeal? Surely more than anything it's the fact that we all harbour hopes of it one day coming true for us. Most of us have an astonishing capacity to hope against hope and are only too happy to have that innate optimism reinforced.

Unfortunately, such tales are usually confined to the realm of fiction, but in our reading, today, we have a rags-to-riches tale of a different sort and one rooted firmly in the world of fact. It concerns not an individual who rises from obscurity but a place – one of the little towns of Judah – its only claim to fame, prior to the birth of Christ, that it had been the birthplace of David; yet this, according to Micah, was where the Messiah would one day be born. Not in Jerusalem, as you might have expected – the holy city and seat of religious and political government – but in the little backwater of Bethlehem. So, what did this mean? Was it just an interesting but ultimately unimportant detail? Taken in isolation we might assume just that, but there are innumerable facts that indicate other-wise. We need only look at the life of Jesus – the person he was, the ministry he exercised and the message he preached – to realise how often God demonstrated strength through weakness: a help-less baby in a manger; a handful of unlikely disciples; the Prince of Peace riding on a donkey; the 'King of the Jews' hanging on a cross. Add to that how God chose Mary to bear his son, a carpenter to share in rearing him, and shepherds to be the first to hear and celebrate the good news, and suddenly that small detail of his birthplace takes on a new significance. Here is yet another example of the way God so often works – choosing not the strong but the weak, not the powerful but the humble, not the influential in the eyes of the world but the small and apparently insignificant.

The message is as true today as it has always been. We may consider ourselves the last person God could have time for. We may count ourselves unworthy of his love and undeserving of his goodness. We may feel that there are countless others more quali- fied than we are, a multitude he would use before ever considering us. Yet, that is to look at the world with our eyes rather than his. The stable of Bethlehem reminds us never to underestimate how much we mean to God and how much he is able to use us.

Second, and equally important, never underestimate what even the smallest word or deed can achieve. Can my stumbling hesitant words of testimony ever communicate the gospel? With God's help, yes! Can my flawed half-hearted service begin to make a differ- ence to someone's life? With God's help, yes! Can my prayers ever actually change anything? With God's help, yes! Can that small gesture, that tiny gift, that lone stand, possibly have any meaning- ful impact in a disbelieving world? With God's help, yes! Our efforts may seem feeble and our resources so small – a meaningless drop in the ocean – but again the message of Bethlehem rings out today: never underestimate what God can do.

Finally, and perhaps most important of all, never underestimate what God is doing now. That is what so many did on the day that Jesus was born. They had looked forward to his coming for so long, yet on that night in Bethlehem most people apparently were unaware of anything happening. While shepherds hurried to the manger and then went on their way rejoicing, for most it was just another day. While God was demonstrating his love as never before, the majority had no inkling of what was taking place. The same can be true for us. For the occasional high spots we have in discipleship – moments like our conversion, baptism or confirma- tion, or times when our prayers are unmistakably answered – there are far more ordinary times, when there is no blinding revela- tion, no clear sense of God's guidance, no sense of anything unusual happening. Yet, God can be at work there nonetheless, working out his purpose though we fail to see it. Never under- estimate, says Bethlehem, the ordinary moments, for God may be more at work there than anywhere!

Do we feel we haven't much to commend ourselves; that we are undeserving of God's love, our gifts so limited that there is little we can do in his service? It's natural that we should, for in human terms it's true, but Christmas reminds us that it's not what *we* think that matters; it's what God thinks, what God *is* and what God is able to do by his sovereign grace.

'From you, Bethlehem of Ephrathah, small though you may be among the clans of Judah, shall emerge one who is to rule in Israel.' A seemingly unimportant detail, but a vital one!

Summary

- We all like to think it's possible for the weak to overcome the strong and for the insignificant to achieve greatness, but more often that not such transformations are the stuff of fiction.
- The prophecy of Micah concerning Bethlehem as the birthplace of the Messiah represents that hope becoming fact.
- Jesus repeatedly demonstrated that God is able to use the ordinary things of life to accomplish the extraordinary.
- Never underestimate how much you mean to God or how he is able to use you in the fulfilment of his purposes.
- Never underestimate what God is doing in your life and the way he is working in the world, however much it may not feel like it.

Discussion

- Are there times when you have surprised yourself by achieving something you thought yourself incapable of? Have others surprised you in a similar way? Do you sometimes underestimate the way God can use others?
- Recall incidents when seeming 'Davids' have overcome 'Goliaths'. What do you think was the key to their success? Can you learn anything from their example?
- Are we all guilty sometimes, even in the Church, of judging strength and success by outside appearances? In what ways do you do this?

Further reading: 1 Corinthians 1:26-29

Brothers and sisters, consider your calling. Not many of you were wise, powerful or influential by human standards. Yet God chose the foolish things of this world to shame the wise, the weak things to shame the strong, and the things considered worthless – indeed, as nothing at all – to bring to nothing those who think they are something, so that no one might boast before God.

Meditation

Bethlehem – not much of a place, is it?
I can't pretend otherwise.
Nothing special about it or unusual,
    just your typical Judean town really,
    a sleepy provincial backwater
    quietly going about its own business.
And why not?
Don't think I'm knocking it –
    quite the opposite –
    it just isn't the sort of place you'd expect to hit the headlines,
    still less to set the world on fire.
Yet, do you know what –
    ever since I passed through last week
    I've had this strange feeling
    that God has put his finger on the place,
    singled it out for a particular purpose,
    a special honour that will give it a place in history for ever.
Yes, ridiculous I know –
    I've told myself that time and time again these last few days –
    but it makes no difference,
    I just can't get the idea out of my head.
It's raised a few eyebrows, I can tell you –
    a right one we've got here,
    that's what people are thinking when I tell them.
And who can blame them?
'Prove it!' they tell me.

'Show us the evidence!'
And of course I can't, for there isn't any;
    just this hunch that God was speaking to me.
Yet before you write the idea off completely,
    stop and think for a minute,
    for is it really so way out as it first sounds?
Wouldn't it actually be typical of the way God so often works –
    confounding our expectations,
    turning our view of the world upside down,
    using the little to accomplish the great,
    the insignificant to achieve the spectacular,
    the humble to astonish the proud?
Remember Moses! Joshua! David!
Remember Egypt! Jericho! Goliath!
Time and again, it's been the same story,
    where God is concerned, small is beautiful.
I may be wrong this time, of course; I accept that.
It could simply be some crazy bee in my bonnet.
But I don't think so.
In fact, the more I think about it,
    the more certain I feel it's the way God will choose –
    surprising us not simply through his coming
    but through the very way he comes.
You may think different; it's up to you –
    keep on looking to Jerusalem if you want to.
But me?
I'm looking to Bethlehem;
    the last place you'd expect, admittedly,
    but in God's eyes, last but not least!

Suggestions for action

- Ask yourself what things you have failed to do because you did not think God could use you. If the opportunity is still open, take the leap of faith.
- Consider your attitude to others, and reassess what God is able to do through them.

Prayer

Sovereign God,
    time and again you have overturned human expectations,
    using the most unlikely of people
    in yet more unlikely surroundings.
You have shown beyond doubt that no situation or person
    is outside the scope of your purpose –
    that you can use each and every one of us.
Teach us, then, to recognise all you would do through us
    and everything you can do through others,
    working in ways we would never dare to contemplate
    and can scarcely even imagine.
Sovereign God,
    you recognise the potential of everyone and everything –
    help us to do the same.
Amen.

Third week after Christmas

An enduring promise

Prayer

Lord,
    teach me to seek thee,
    and reveal thyself to me when I seek thee.
For I cannot seek thee unless thou teach me,
    nor find thee except thou reveal thyself.
Let me seek thee in longing,
    let me long for thee in seeking;
    let me find thee in love,
    and love thee in finding.
Amen.

Prayer of St Ambrose

Introduction

'Seek and you will find.' At least that's what Jesus tells us, but it's not always quite so straightforward as it may sound. Take, for example, the Christmas stories, and two of the journeys we read of there. First, there were the shepherds, their search a short and simple one: they went and found the baby lying in a manger, just as the angel had told them. For the magi, though, it was a different story; theirs a long and tiring journey calling for patience and determination – a journey that brought them first to Jerusalem and only then, after careful enquiry, on to Bethlehem. They arrived not at the stable, but at a house, presumably Jesus and his family having taken up lodging there; and they greeted not a baby but a child, possibly as much as two years old.

Did they wonder sometimes whether it was worth continuing? Did they fear, perhaps, that they had taken a wrong turning somewhere, or misunderstood the signs? Did they even question whether they would reach their destination at all? We will never know. What we do know is that their search, however long it took, proved successful, God leading them to the place where the child lay. So also, if we are ready to seek, will he lead us until we discover the reality of his love in Christ for ourselves. That is not just an idle hope; it's a promise!

Quiz
See Appendix 1, page 75.

Reading: Matthew 2:1-12

After Jesus had been born in Bethlehem of Judea, during the reign of King Herod, wise men arrived in Jerusalem from the East, asking, 'Where is the one born the king of the Jews? For we saw his star in the East, and so have come to pay him homage.' On hearing this, King Herod was alarmed, and all Jerusalem with him; and, having assembled all the chief priests and scribes of the people, he asked them where the Messiah was to be born. They told him, 'In Bethlehem of Judea; for so it has been written by the prophet: "And you, Bethlehem, in the land of Judah, are by no means least among the rulers of Judah; for from you shall come a ruler who is to shepherd my people Israel."' Then Herod secretly summoned the wise men and ascertained the exact time the star had appeared. Then he sent them to Bethlehem, saying, 'Go and search thoroughly for the child; and when you find him, report back to me so that I also may pay him homage.' After listening to the king, they set out; and, sure enough, the star they had seen dawning in the East went ahead of them, until it stopped over the place where the child was. When they saw that the star had stopped, they were beside themselves with joy. Entering the house, they saw the child with Mary his mother, and, prostrating themselves, they paid him homage. Then, opening their treasure chests, they offered him gifts – gold, frankincense and myrrh. Finally, having been warned in a dream not to return to Herod, they returned to their own country by another route.

Comment

I was on my way to lead worship at a church near London, conscious that it was an important engagement. One of my college lecturers had once been minister at the church, and my job was to represent the college and further its work. I'd left nothing to chance, catching a train half an hour before I needed to, just in case it might be running late, but no, I needn't have worried; the journey had been smooth and the station was in sight. Congratulating myself on my efficient planning, I got up and reached for the door – then looked out in disbelief as, instead of slowing down, the train picked up speed, positively thundering through the station and on its way. Three stations later it stopped, and frantically I jumped on to a train pulling out in the other direction. Thankfully this one called at all stations, and at last, panting for breath, dripping with sweat and red as a beetroot, I blundered into the church, just in time to take a swig of water and launch into one of the worst sermons I've ever preached! As a member of the congregation caustically remarked after the service, 'Better late than never!'

It was my own fault, of course – I'd failed to allow for a revised Sunday timetable – but that only added to my humiliation. Most of us will be spared such a public humiliation, but we will all know that awful feeling of seeing the minutes tick away and fearing we are going to be too late. We race to the bus stop, just in time to see the service we wanted pulling away. We dash round to the shops, only to get there as the doors are being locked. We work against the clock to meet a deadline, only to miss the last post.

Yet, painful though such times may be, the magi must have suffered infinitely more, for they were hurrying not to catch a bus or keep an appointment, but to share in an historic event, one they considered to be of global significance. No doubt they started off enthusiastically enough, but as days turned to weeks, and the weeks to months, increasingly they must have feared they would be too late; that if and when they arrived the celebrations would long since be over? To arrive in Jerusalem and find that no one knew what they were talking about must have seemed like the final straw, their whole venture a wild goose chase. Yet they kept on following the star; kept on trusting and hoping, until at last they came and found the child – late perhaps, but better late than never! It may have taken them longer than the shepherds, they may have missed the initial excitement of his birth, the journey may have been tortuous and demanding such that they thought they would never make it, but the important thing was that they had come. They had persevered in their personal pilgrimage, refusing to lose heart and accept defeat, and finally they experienced the reality of God's gift in Christ for themselves!

For us, too, the search may not be easy. We may look but fail to find, unable to get past our doubts and questions, the things we cannot make sense of, the obstacles that stand in the way of faith. We may set out on the journey of discipleship, only to lose our way, one moment thinking we have arrived and the next unsure where to turn next. We may have put off the journey, reluctant to make a decision, afraid of committing ourselves, and now we may feel we have left it too late. Whatever the case, the journey of the magi calls us to think again, for it reminds us that God's promise is never exhausted – that all who seek him shall find.

If we need convincing further, look again at the extraordinary testimony of the apostle Paul concerning his own coming to faith in Christ: 'He appeared to Peter, then to the Twelve, and after that to five hundred of the brothers at the same time. Then he appeared to James, then to all the apostles, and finally he appeared to me also, as to one abnormally born' (1 Corinthians 15:5-8). Paul, the last of the apostles to come to faith, and in his own estimation the least of them; the one who for so long had opposed Christ, fought against him, resisted his challenge, until at last he could hold out no longer. If anyone was unworthy, it was him; if anyone had missed his chance, again it was him; if anyone was too late, surely once more it was him; but even he, the most unlikely of candidates, came to discover the reality of Christ for himself! Late, but better late than never!

Christmas may be over and forgotten for another year. It may be time to take down the cards and decorations, and get the house back to normal, but the truth at the heart of this season is one we can celebrate today and every day! A Saviour has been born to us who is Christ the Lord; a Saviour who invites you and me and everyone to know him and experience his love for ourselves. Our journey may have started or it may have only just begun, but we have his word: 'Seek and you will find.' Like all God's promises, it is an assurance that endures for ever.

Summary

- Journeys do not always work out as we planned. We can wonder sometimes if we will reach our destination at all, or if it will be too late when we do.
- Unlike the shepherds, the magi's journey must have been long and difficult, calling for faith and perseverance, yet ultimately they reached their goal.
- We may feel sometimes that our search for Christ is in vain, or that somehow we have lost our way. The story of the apostle Paul reminds us that no one is outside of God's love and that it is never too late to turn to him.
- The message of Christmas is a message for every day. Seek, and we will discover the reality of God in Christ for ourselves. We have his enduring promise.

Discussion

- What experiences have you had of being late for something or someone?
- How did you come to faith? Was your journey a natural progression or a long and arduous search? Is there a sense in which we are all still searching?
- Have there been times when you have lost your way or felt like giving up?

Further reading: Jeremiah 29:12b-14a

If you appeal to me in prayer, I will hear you; if you search for me, you will find me; if you seek me with all your heart, I will ensure you find me, says the Lord.

Meditation

Well, we made it at last,
    after all the setbacks,
    all the frustration,
    we finally found the one we were looking for –
    our journey over,
    the quest completed.
And I can't tell you how relieved we were.
You see, we'd begun to fear we'd be too late,
    the time for celebration long since past
    by the time we eventually arrived.
It was that business in Jerusalem which caused the delay,
    all the waiting around
    whilst Herod and his entourage rummaged around
    trying to discover what we were on about.
They were unsettled for some reason,
    taken aback, it seemed, by the news we brought,
    apparently unaware a king had been born among them.
A rival claimant, they must have thought,
    and who could tell what trouble that might stir up?
Anyway, they pointed us in the right direction if nothing else,
    but we'd wasted time there we could ill afford,
    and although the star reappeared to lead us again,
    we were almost falling over ourselves with haste
    by the time we reached Bethlehem.
It was all quiet,
    just as we feared –
    no crowds,
    no family bustling around offering their congratulations,
    no throng of excited visitors,
    just an ordinary house –
    so ordinary we thought we'd gone to the wrong place.
But we went in anyway,
    and the moment we saw the child, we knew he was the one –
    not just the king of the Jews,
    but a prince among princes,

a ruler among rulers,
a King of kings!
We were late,
much later than intended,
the journey far more difficult than we ever expected,
but it was worth the effort,
worth struggling on,
for like they say, 'Better late than never!'

Suggestions for action

- If you feel you have left it too late to respond to Christ, think again.
- If you feel you have lost your way, ask God for guidance and renew your search.
- If you feel you have arrived at your destination, remind your-self that there is always more to learn; that in this life we can only ever see in part.

Prayer

Gracious God,
such is your love for us that you go on calling,
however long it takes for us to respond,
and you go on leading,
however tortuous our journey of faith may be.
We may put off a decision,
keep you at arms length –
still you are there to guide,
striving to draw us to yourself.
We may encounter obstacles that impede our progress,
that cause us to go astray,
that obscure the truth,
yet always you are there to show us the way forward.
Teach us that your love will never let us go,
and so help us to make our response
and bring our lives to you in joyful homage,
knowing that you will continue to lead us until our journey's end.
Through Jesus Christ our Lord.
Amen.

Fourth week after Christmas

An answered promise

Prayer

Lord, when I think only of my own wants and desires,
    I am impatient to have them satisfied;
    yet in my heart I know that such satisfaction
    will crumble to dust.
Give me the spirit of hope
    which can enable me to want what you want,
    and to wait patiently on your time
    in the knowledge that in you alone
    is found lasting pleasure.
Amen.

Mozarabic Sacramentary (third century)

Introduction

It is not just faith in oneself that can take a knock as the years go by; it is faith in God's promises as well. As another natural catastrophe strikes or another country is plunged into violent conflict, as another friend dies before their time, or another person is raped, mugged or murdered, it becomes increasingly difficult to reconcile the harsh realities of life with the idea of a God of love. The fact that society as a whole generally dismisses any talk of God makes it all the harder to keep on believing; few able to withstand the drip-drip effect of scorn and scepticism or sheer disinterest. Yet the example of both Simeon and the prophetess Anna, urges us to trust despite appearances, confident that God is at work and that, in the fullness of time, his purpose will be fulfilled. Anna had the courage to stay true to her faith despite outward appearances. Have we?

Quiz
See Appendix 1, page 75.

Reading: Luke 2:25-38
There was a man in Jerusalem called Simeon who was upright and devout, eagerly awaiting the consolation of Israel, and the Holy Spirit dwelt upon him. The Spirit had disclosed to him that he would not taste death before he had seen the Lord's Messiah. Led by the Spirit, Simeon entered the temple; and when Jesus' parents brought in their child to honour the customs of the Law, Simeon cradled him in his arms and praised God, saying, 'Master, you are now dismissing your servant in peace, according to your promise. With my own eyes I have seen the salvation you have prepared before all the world – a light that will reveal you to the Gentiles and bring glory to your people Israel.' The child's parents were stunned at these words concerning him. Then Simeon blessed them and said to his mother Mary, 'This child is ordained to be a sign that many will reject; one through whom the inner thoughts of many will be revealed and who will pierce your own soul. Many in Israel will stand or fall because of him.'

In similar fashion, there was a prophetess called Anna, a daughter of Phanuel of the tribe of Asher. She was of a great age, having lived with her husband seven years after the day of her marriage, and then as a widow until the age of 84, during the latter time not once having left the temple but having served God there through prayer and fasting night and day. Entering at that very moment, she gave thanks to God and spoke of the child to all those in Jerusalem who were waiting for redemption.

Comment
Have you ever had the misfortune of needing to go to a hospital casualty department?

If you have, then you will know how frustrating an experience it can be. You arrive there moaning in agony, blood pouring from a wound, your arm broken in five places, only to be ushered to a seat and told that someone will see to you shortly. Were that true, it wouldn't be too bad, except that in hospital jargon 'shortly' has a very different meaning to that usually associated with the term. One hour goes by, two, even three, and still you find yourself waiting to be seen to 'shortly'. Eventually it is not pain you want to cry out with so much as sheer boredom and frustration. It gives the word 'patient' a whole new meaning!

Not, of course, that hospitals are the only places where we can be kept waiting. Try driving to work through a busy city, or ringing a customer helpline when the appliance you've just bought has gone wrong, or, worst of all, if recent years are anything to go by, attempting to travel anywhere by rail, and you will know exactly what it means to have your patience tested to the limit. There comes a point when we despair of ever reaching our destination or achieving our goal. All of which gives us some insight into the astonishing patience of the two people in our reading today. They appear on centre stage just for a moment, but it is well worth reflecting a little more deeply on their story, and, in particular, on the story of Anna.

On the surface what we see in her is a somewhat eccentric old lady who had spent the majority of her 84 years worshipping and praying in the temple, never once leaving it in all that time. It is hard not to feel there is something intensely tragic about that picture, for, however much she may have been devoting her life to God, there is a sense in which she was also turning her back on the very life given. So why had she chosen such a strange and reclusive life, turning her back on the world beyond? The answer is given in that one poignant detail: 'She was of a great age, having lived with her husband seven years after the day of her marriage, and then as a widow until the age of 84' (Luke 2:36). In relation to the gospel story, it is a small and almost incidental detail but, in terms of Anna's life, it is surely the determining factor. Here was a woman who had suffered personal tragedy of the cruellest kind, widowed while she was still young, her life turned upside down by the trauma and associated heartbreak of bereavement after just seven years of married life. That would have been a hard enough experience to bear at any time, but in the society of Anna's day it meant being left vulnerable and alone in a ruthlessly male-dominated world with no one to provide for her or look out for her interests. For Anna, without doubt, bereavement must have been a time when her world fell apart; when everything she had trusted in for security and happiness had been snatched from her. Everything, that is, except God. He was the one unchanging certainty in the chaos and confusion of life that she could hold on to, knowing that though all else might fail, he would not. Even though she must have found her husband's death hard to reconcile with her faith; even though she must have asked God innumerable times, 'Why me? Why him?'; even though she must have felt sometimes like blaming God for all her troubles, she held on.

What was it, though, that she held on to so firmly? Was it the comfort of worship and ritual in temple? That may have been part of it. Was it the teaching and guidance offered by the teachers of the law? That also may have helped. Was it the companionship of the crowds flocking to visit the temple? Certainly that too may have been a comfort. Yet those, finally, were all incidental to what really sustained her, and that, quite simply, was her faith in God's purpose, for Anna believed he had something more for her to look forward to in life. Despite all she had endured, she was convinced that grief, pain, hurt and sorrow were not to be the final word. Though the wound of her loss must still often have ached within, the memory rubbing raw, she believed God would yet bless her. There had been a time to weep but there would also be a time to laugh; the time for mourning would ultimately give way to a time for dancing. That was why she prayed and fasted, why she remained night and day in the temple – because she believed God had called her to see the day of Christ's coming, and, more importantly, that she would be privileged to make that coming known!

Yet, how hard it must have been to keep on believing that as week followed week, month followed month and year followed year; as the first year passed, the fifth, tenth, twentieth, fiftieth, and still there was no sign of the promise being realised. How hard it must have been not to conclude the waiting was in vain, that what she was waiting for was nothing but an empty delusion, never going to happen. How hard not to lose patience! Perhaps she did lose patience sometimes – we can never know. Perhaps she did find it harder week in, week out, to worship and pray with the same enthusiasm. Perhaps she started, in time, to get frustrated and angry with God, as nothing seemed to happen. Perhaps she even began to lose her faith. Who can say? Yet whether she did or not, Anna faithfully kept on along the path she had chosen, until at last her trust was rewarded. Somehow, when she saw the child Jesus brought into the temple, she knew it was the moment she had been waiting for, the end of her long vigil.

Here, in a nutshell, we see one of the key themes at the heart of Advent: the need for patience. 'Christ has died, Christ is risen, Christ will come again' – words so often spoken at the Lord's Table that echo the familiar Advent refrain, 'Come, Lord, come!' We don't just mean come again in glory, though that is central; we mean come now, to our lives, to our church, to our world. Only it gets harder to go on believing he will come, let alone that he is with us here and now in the daily routine of life. As we look at the world with all its need and pain, evil and suffering; as we look at the Church with all its weaknesses, faults, unwieldy structures and divisions; as we look at ourselves with all our fears, doubts, faults and weaknesses, we can begin to wonder: What is God playing at? Where is his kingdom? It's hard to go on trusting and hoping when nothing seems to happen; hard not to let the doubts creep in and our enthusiasm wane. None of us is immune from that slow and subtle erosion of our faith.

The story of Anna, like that of Simeon, reminds us that God is faithful and will always finally honour his promise. It calls us to look forward in faith, confident that one day his kingdom shall come and his will be done! It urges us never to lose heart or give up, never to be taken in by appearances, however hopeless they may seem. We may find ourselves asking sometimes if God has heard our prayer or cares about our situation, even if he is there at all. Anna's testimony assures us that he is, encapsulating the Advent and Christmas message that God is faithful, and that what he has promised he will surely do!

Summary

- Life often calls for patience but it is hard sometimes not to lose heart.
- Both Simeon and Anna had waited many years for the Advent of the Messiah, years that must have tested their faith to the limit, but finally their patient trust was rewarded.
- It's hard to continue believing in the promises of God when so much in life seems to contradict them. We can all too easily lose faith in the dawn of his kingdom.
- Like Anna and Simeon we need to hold on, despite appearances. In this life or the next, God will honour his promises.

Discussion

- Does your faith in God's purpose burn as brightly as it once did? Have you allowed disappointment to blunt your vision?
- What might cause God to delay the fulfilment of his promises?
- How realistic is it to expect those promises to be fulfilled in this life? Is there a danger of emphasising the present at the cost of the future, or vice versa?

Further reading: Romans 8:18-25

I believe that we cannot begin to compare our present sufferings to the glory that God holds in store for us. All creation yearns with eager expectation for the appearance of the children of God. It was subjected to frustration not by its own volition but by the will of the one who so made it, but who also gives the hope that creation itself will be set free from its current bondage to decay and so obtain the glorious freedom of the children of God. We know that until now the whole creation has been groaning with the pangs of childbirth. Not just creation but us too, for, having the first fruits of the Spirit, we sigh inwardly, longing for adoption as God's children and the redemption of our bodies. We are saved by hope. Hope in what is seen is not hope, for why hope in what we can see? We hope, though, for what we cannot see, and we wait for it patiently.

Meditation

I really felt I'd missed it,
    truthfully.
I mean, I wasn't just old,
    I was ancient!
And still there was no sign of the Messiah,
    no hint of his coming.
I began to wonder whether all those years of praying and fasting
    had been worth it,
    or simply one almighty waste of time.
I doubted everything,
    questioned everything,
    despite my outward piety.
Why hadn't God answered my prayers?
Why hadn't he rewarded my faithfulness?
Why believe when it didn't seem to make a scrap of difference?
I still kept up the facade mind you –
    still spoke excitedly of the future
    and of everything that God would do –
    but I didn't have much faith in it,
    not after so many disappointments.
Until that day when,
    hobbling back through the temple after yet more prayers,
    suddenly I saw him,
    God's promised Messiah.
Don't ask me how I knew,
    I just did,
    without any shadow of a doubt,
    and it was the most wonderful moment of my life,
    a privilege beyond words.
It taught me something, that experience.
It taught me there is always reason to hope,
    no matter how futile it seems.
It taught me to go on expecting,
    despite all the blows life may dish out –

never to give up,
or let go,
or lose heart.
It taught me that God's love is never exhausted,
however much it may feel like it.
I nearly lost sight of all that.
I was right on the edge,
teetering on the brink,
fearing God had passed me by.
But he'd saved the best till last,
and I know now,
even though the waiting is over,
that there's more to come,
more to expect,
more to celebrate;
that, though my life is nearly at an end,
it has only just begun!

Suggestions for action

- Think again about those hopes you have given up on, recognising that God's timing is not the same as your own.
- Pray for patience and faith.
- Ask if there is something you should be doing to help bring God's promises to fulfilment. If there is, do it!

Prayer

Loving God,
as the years go by and life drifts on,
we find it hard sometimes to keep faith as fresh as it once was.
As we face life's repeated disappointments,
and as prayer after prayer seems to go unanswered,
so faith falters,
the dreams of youth dulled by the reality of experience.
Yet, you tell us through Jesus never to stop looking forward
and never to stop believing in the future.

Help us, then, to continue trusting in the victory of your love
    and the coming of your kingdom,
    despite everything that seems to deny it.
Renew our faith, revive our hope,
    restore our trust, rekindle our vision,
    and so may we serve you in quiet confidence,
    this day and always.
Through Jesus Christ our Lord.
Amen.

Appendix 1

Quizzes

The following quizzes are not designed as a test of the participants' IQ but as a means of breaking the ice and stimulating conversation. Each is loosely based around the theme of the session, and so can be channelled towards further discussion.

First week of Advent: A disturbing promise

Many across the years have painted a picture of what life in the future might be like, or have even claimed the ability to foresee what the future holds. Some have been well wide of the mark; the vision of others is chillingly disturbing in its credibility.

1. In which book do we read that 'Big brother is watching you'?

2. Who wrote the classic novel _Brave New World_?

3. Which science fiction story caused mass panic when it was broadcast on the radio in dramatised form?

4. Which celebrated astrologer set himself up as a 'prophet' in 1547?

5. Which woman was employed as a 'fortune-teller' in the early days of the National Lottery?

6. Which annual publication makes predictions concerning key events in the year ahead?

7. Who wrote _2001: a Space Odyssey_?

8. Which economics textbook, published in the 1960s, caused widespread consternation with its warning of ecological disaster unless patterns of consumption were drastically reduced?

Second week of Advent: A sure and certain promise

The pages of the Bible are packed full of promises; many of them already realised, many others awaiting fulfilment. Below are just a few examples.

1. Who was promised by God that all the world would be blessed through his offspring?
2. Whom did God call to lead the Israelites out of Egypt and to the brink of the Promised Land?
3. In which book do we read of God's promise that 'the wolf shall live with the lamb, the leopard shall lie down with the kid'?
4. Which reluctant prophet was reassured by the promise of God to give him the words to speak when he needed to speak them?
5. Who was told he would not taste death until he had seen the Messiah?
6. Where do we read about Jesus' promise that God will send us an Advocate or Comforter?
7. Who did Jesus promise, in the so-called Beatitudes, will be called children of God?
8. What gift does Jesus promise us that the world cannot give?

Third week of Advent: An incredible promise

Across the years, there have always been those ready to attempt what others have dismissed as impossible. Below are some of those who succeeded in reaching their goal.

1. Who were the first two people to conquer Mount Everest?
2. What was the date of the first landing on the moon?
3. Who was the first person to walk to the South Pole?
4. What time did Roger Bannister record when he became the first person officially to run a four-minute mile?
5. Who completed golf's Grand Slam of majors with victory at the US Masters in 2001?

6. Which doctor performed the first successful human heart transplant?
7. Who was the first person to swim the English Channel?
8. In which year did Christopher Columbus make his epic journey to the West Indies?

Fourth week of Advent: A demanding promise

For many people, their promise of loyalty to a person, conviction or cause has meant immense sacrifice, even to the point of death. The following are all people who paid the ultimate price for staying true to the things they believed in.

1. Which bishops' devotion to the principles of the Reformation cost them their lives under Mary Tudor?
2. Which biblical character's final loyalty to his father over his friend was to cost him his life?
3. Which non-violent campaigner was assassinated by a Hindu extremist?
4. Which Archbishop of Canterbury was assassinated in 1170?
5. Which civil rights campaigner was assassinated in 1968?
6. Which German theologian and pastor was hanged shortly before the end of the Second World War, following his resistance to Hitler?
7. Which translator of the Bible into English was executed in 1536?
8. Which Lord Chancellor of England was executed for his opposition to the plans of the then king?

First week after Christmas: A personal promise

Promises are made for various reasons: sometimes for political expediency, sometimes as a legal requirement, sometimes as a rallying cry, or sometimes as part of an organisation. The questions below explore some of the personal promises that have been or might be made.

1. Which US president declared 'Watch my lips: no more taxes' and then put up taxes to unprecedented levels?
2. Which British Prime Minister went down in history for ill-advisedly promising 'peace in our time'?
3. What promises are the Scouts asked to make?
4. What promise are witnesses asked to make in court?
5. What oath is associated with the medical profession?
6. What promise was David Shayler accused of breaking?
7. Who promised, 'We shall fight on the beaches, we shall fight on the landing grounds, we shall fight in the fields and in the streets, we shall fight in the hills; we shall never surrender'?
8. Who is attributed with coining the saying 'They shall not pass', subsequently taken up by Republicans in the Spanish Civil War?

Second week after Christmas: A surprising promise

1. Which number is the bigger – 16,777,216 or 8^8?
2. If you were to pass on a message to two people, and ask each of them to pass it on to two other people, asking them to ask two other people and so on, how many people would get to hear the message, after it has been passed on through ten complete cycles?
3. Which small town in the early 1800s grew into Britain's third largest city?
4. Who went from being a computer 'nerd' barely 20 years ago to become one of the world's richest people today?
5. Who grew up as a butcher's son in Suffolk before rising to become a Cardinal during the reign of King Henry VIII?
6. What distinction is held by Karol Jozef Wojtyla?
7. Which comic actor began life as Arthur Stanley Jefferson?
8. Which celebrated actor was born Maurice Micklewhite in the East End of London?

Third week after Christmas: An enduring promise

1. Who scored the goals that won the European Cup for Manchester United in injury time?

2. How long did the latest-ever postal delivery actually take to arrive?

3. Which former James Bond actor was finally honoured with a knighthood in 2001?

4. Which British tennis player achieved success at Wimbledon in the year of the Queen's Silver Jubilee?

5. Which popular modern-day author had her first novel published in her mid-70s?

6. When did the Second World War end for Private Teruo Naka-mura?

7. How many games did it take Pancho Gonzalez to beat Charlie Pasarell in the longest ever men's singles match at Wimbledon?

8. Who had a Number One hit single in the UK at the age of 67 years and 10 months?

Fourth week after Christmas: An answered promise

Delays and frustrating periods of waiting are a part of life; a fact borne out by the number of sayings and proverbs on the theme of patience. Can you fill in the missing words below to complete each maxim?

1. A __ kettle __ __

2. All __ come __ those who __

3. __ is a __

4. __ wasn't __ in a __

5. We must learn to __ before we can __

6. __ but __ wins __ __

7. Where there's __ there's __

8. __ is another __

Appendix 2

Quiz answers

First week of Advent: A disturbing promise

1. *1984*
2. Aldous Huxley
3. *The War of the Worlds*
4. Nostradamus
5. Mystic Meg
6. *Whitaker's Almanack*
7. Arthur C. Clarke
8. *Limits to Growth*

Second week of Advent: A sure and certain promise

1. Abraham (Genesis 15:1-6)
2. Moses (Exodus 3:3-15)
3. Isaiah (Isaiah 11:6)
4. Jeremiah (Jeremiah 1:4-10)
5. Simeon (Luke 2:25-35)
6. John 14:15-26
7. The peacemakers (Matthew 5:9)
8. Peace (John 14:27)

Third week of Advent: An incredible promise

1. Sir Edmund Hillary and Tenzing Norgay, in 1953
2. 20 July 1969
3. Roald Amundsen
4. 3 minutes 59.4 seconds
5. Tiger Woods

6. Dr Christiaan Barnard
7. Matthew Webb, in 1875
8. 1492

Fourth week of Advent: A demanding promise

1. Bishops Latimer, Ridley and Cranmer
2. Jonathan, the son of Saul and friend of David
3. Mahatma Gandhi
4. Thomas à Becket
5. Martin Luther King
6. Dietrich Bonhoeffer
7. William Tyndale
8. Sir Thomas More

First week after Christmas: A personal promise

1. George Bush (father of George W. Bush)
2. Sir Anthony Eden
3. On my honour, I promise that I will do my best to do my duty to God and to the Queen, to help other people and to keep the Scout Law.
4. I promise to tell the truth, the whole truth and nothing but the truth.
5. The Hippocratic Oath
6. The Official Secrets Act
7. Sir Winston Churchill
8. Marshall Pétain, at the battle of Verdun in 1916

Second week after Christmas: A surprising promise

1. Neither. They are exactly the same!
2. 2048
3. Manchester

4. Bill Gates
5. Cardinal Wolsey
6. He is the first Pole to become pope (Pope John Paul II)
7. Stan Laurel (of Laurel and Hardy fame)
8. Michael Caine

Third week after Christmas: An enduring promise

1. Teddy Sheringham and Ole Gunnar Solskjaer
2. A letter sent by Mr J. F. Brown of Hampstead finally reached its destination 38 years, seven months, five weeks and one day late, by which time its intended recipient was dead!
3. Sean Connery
4. Virginia Wade
5. Mary Wesley
6. 10 March 1974. Stationed on the remote island of Lubang in the Philippines in 1944, he waged a lone guerrilla campaign, killing at least 50 Filipinos. He only finally surrendered when his old commanding officer, Major Taniguchi, by then a bookseller back in Japan, was specially flown in to confirm the order.
7. 112 games, in 1969
8. Louis Armstrong, with 'What a wonderful world'

Fourth week after Christmas: An answered promise

1. A *watched* kettle *never boils*
2. All *things* come *to* those who *wait*
3. *Patience* is a *virtue*
4. *Rome* wasn't *built* in a *day*
5. We must learn to *walk* before we can *run*
6. *Slow* but *sure* wins *the day*
7. Where there's *life* there's *hope*
8. *Tomorrow* is another *day*

Appendix 3

Suggested music

As a closing reflection for each session

'May the Lord bless you' 3.27 (Margaret Rizza, *Chants and Songs*)

First week of Advent: A disturbing promise

'Come, Lord' 3.58 (Margaret Rizza, *Fountain of Life*)
'O come, O come, Emmanuel' 5.44 (performed by Rick Wakeman)
'Put your law within my mind' 3.36 (from *Hopesongs*, composed by Rick Wakeman and Howard Prior)

Second week of Advent: A sure and certain promise

'Morning has broken' 3.25 (performed by Rick Wakeman)
'Come, Lord' 3.58 (Margaret Rizza, from *Fountain of Life*)
'Benedictus' 7.06 (Margaret Rizza, from *River of Peace*)

Third week of Advent: An incredible promise

'May the Lord bless you' 3.27 (Margaret Rizza, *Chants and Songs*)
'O Lord, my heart is not proud' 7.43 (Margaret Rizza, *Fountain of Life*)
'Christus natus est' 5.34 (Margaret Rizza, *Fire of Love*)

Fourth week of Advent: A demanding promise

'The mother of Jesus' 3.30 (sung by Chichester Cathedral Choir)
'Mary had a baby' 1.57 (sung by Chichester Cathedral Choir)
'Silent, surrendered' 4.22 (Margaret Rizza, from *Fountain of Life*)

First week after Christmas: A personal promise

'As Joseph was a-walking' 3.29 (Margaret Rizza, *River of Peace*)
'Like a candle flame' 2.36 (Graham Kendrick, from *The Graham Kendrick Christmas Collection*)
'Lord of my life' 5.06 (Margaret Rizza, *Fountain of Life*)

Second week after Christmas: A surprising promise

'Lovely in your littleness' 4.10 (Margaret Rizza, *Chants and Songs*)
'What kind of greatness?' 4.52 (Graham Kendrick, from *The Graham Kendrick Christmas Collection*)
'Tonight' 4.35 (Graham Kendrick, from *The Graham Kendrick Christmas Collection*)

Third week after Christmas: An enduring promise

'Endlessly searching' 5.04 (Chris Bowater, *The Resource for Small Group Worship*, Album 2)
'I wonder as I wander' 2.34 (sung by Chichester Cathedral Choir)
'The Pilgrim Carol' 2.30 (sung by Chichester Cathedral Choir)

Fourth week after Christmas: An answered promise

'Song of the angels' 4.19 (Margaret Rizza, *River of Peace*)
'In the Lord is my joy' 3.32 (Margaret Rizza, *Chants and Songs*)
'Veni, lumen cordium' 4.05 (Margaret Rizza, *Chants and Songs*)

Acknowledgements

The Collect for Advent 2 on page 17 is taken from *The Alternative Service Book,* © 1980 The Central Board of Finance of the Church of England.

The prayer on page 25 is taken from *The Daily Office (Revised)*.

Every effort has been made to trace the owners of copyright material and we hope that no copyright has been infringed. Pardon is sought and apology made if the contrary be the case, and a correction will be made in any reprint of this book